SCHOLASTIC

Read & Write Booklets

Thanksgiving

BY ALYSE SWEENEY

NEW YORK • TORONTO • LONDON • AUCKLAND • SYDNEY

MEXICO CITY • NEW DELHI • HONG KONG • BUENOS AIRES

Teaching *Resources*

Written by Alyse Sweeney
Edited by Immacula A. Rhodes
Cover design Brian LaRossa
Interior illustrations by Anne Kennedy
Interior design by Kathy Massaro

ISBN-13: 978-0-545-23697-3
ISBN-10: 0-545-23697-5

1 2 3 4 5 6 7 8 9 10   40   17 16 15 14 13 12 11 10

Contents

Read & Write Booklets

Introduction

Who were the Pilgrims? What was life like for the Pilgrims and Wampanoag? What was the First Thanksgiving like? How did Thanksgiving become a holiday? Children will learn the answers to these questions—and so much more—in these interactive, motivating booklets. Best of all, completing and personalizing the booklets gives your budding readers and writers a satisfying sense of accomplishment!

Read & Write Booklets: Thanksgiving features ten booklets and three graphic organizers. The booklets include nonfiction features such as the following to help strengthen children's reading skills:

❉ engaging illustrations that closely match the text

❉ headings, captions, labels, and diagrams

❉ writing prompts that connect to text and invite children to analyze and reflect on what they read

❉ drawing prompts to help children express their thoughts

As children read and complete the booklets, they build comprehension and content knowledge. The booklets invite children to reflect on their reading, think critically, and share their thoughts and opinions in writing. In addition, the graphic organizers help children analyze, synthesize, and compare what they learn about this important holiday.

Connection to the Standards

These booklets are designed to meet the following standards outlined by Mid-continent Research for Education and Learning (McREL), an organization that collects and synthesizes national and state standards.

Reading

● Uses reading skills and strategies to understand and interpret informational texts

● Understands the main idea and supporting details in text

● Summarizes information found in text (retells in own words)

● Relates new information to prior knowledge and experience

● Understands structural patterns or organizations in informational texts (chronological, logical, or sequential order; compare-and-contrast; cause-and-effect)

SOURCE: Kendall, J. S., & Marzano, R. J. (2004). *Content knowledge: A compendium of standards and benchmarks for K–12 education.* Aurora, CO: Mid-continent Research for Education and Learning. Online database: http://www.mcrel.org/standards-benchmarks/

Writing

● Uses the general skills and strategies of the writing process, including drawings, to express thoughts, feelings, and ideas

● Uses grammatical and mechanical conventions in writing

History

● Knows the cultural similarities and differences between families now and in the past

● Understands the daily life of a colonial community

● Understands the culture of early Native Americans

● Understands the reasons that Americans celebrate certain national holidays

Using The Booklets

The booklets are designed for flexible use. You can follow the guidelines below for using the booklets in the classroom, or adapt the ideas to better meet children's needs.

- ✺ **Activate Prior Knowledge:** Introduce each booklet with a discussion to activate children's prior knowledge. Invite children to share what they know about the topic. Then ask them to tell what they think they'll learn from the booklet.

- ✺ **Walk Through the Booklet:** Before reading each booklet, walk through the pages with children. Point out the nonfiction features, such as headings, captions, and labels. Also, show children where any writing and drawing prompts are throughout the booklet.

- ✺ **Read, Write, Draw, and Learn:** Read and discuss the text together. Point out new and content-related vocabulary words as you come to them. As you read, raise questions about the information being shared. Work with children to generate possible responses to each writing prompt. Then talk about what students learned, what they want to know more about, and any information that surprised them.

- ✺ **Share:** After children complete their booklets, invite them to share their written responses with classmates. Draw attention to the similarities and differences in their responses. Be sure to send the booklets home for children to share with their families!

Using the Graphic Organizers

Use the graphic organizers (pages 6–8) to help children organize and summarize what they have learned. Here are some booklets that you can use with each graphic organizer:

- ✺ **Ask and Answer Questions:** all booklets

- ✺ **Sequence Events:** *Voyage on the* Mayflower, *The First Thanksgiving,* and *Our Thanksgiving Holiday*

- ✺ **Compare and Contrast:** *Life in a Pilgrim Village; Life in a Wampanoag Homesite; The First Thanksgiving; A Thanksgiving Meal: 1621 and Today; Our Thanksgiving Holiday; Giving Thanks;* and *My Thanksgiving Day*

Assembling the Booklets

It works well to assemble the booklets together as a class. You might make one in advance to use as a model when introducing the booklet to students.

Directions:

 Carefully remove the perforated pages from the book.

 Make double-sided copies of each page on standard 8 1/2-by 11-inch paper.

 Fold each page in half along the solid line.

 Place the pages in numerical order and staple along the spine.

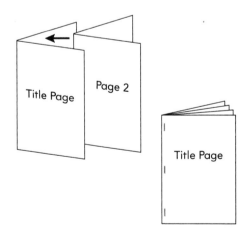

Tɪᴘ: You may want to have children fill in their booklets before stapling them. This way the center pages will lie flat while children write in their responses.

Name _____ Date _____

Book Title _____

Write what you want to know before you read the book.

After reading, write what you learned.

What I Want to Know	What I Learned

Name _____ Date _____

Book Title _____

Pick four events from the book. Write them in order below.

First, _____

_____

_____

Then, _____

_____

_____

Next, _____

_____

_____

Finally, _____

_____

_____

Name _____ Date _____

Book Title(s) _____

I am comparing

and

This is one way they are alike:

_____

_____

_____

This is one way they are different:

_____

_____

_____

Read & Write Booklets: Thanksgiving © 2010 by Scholastic Teaching Resources

Who Were the Pilgrims?

by _____

Searching for a Better Life

What was life like for the Pilgrims before they moved to America?

_____

_____

_____

Write one reason why the Pilgrims moved to America.

_____

_____

_____

Life in England

The Pilgrims were from England. King James said that everyone in the country had to belong to his church. The Pilgrims had different beliefs. They did not want to belong to the Church of England.

King James

Life in America would be hard at first. The Pilgrims knew that they would have to build homes. They would have to learn how to farm the land. Even so, they believed that life would be better for them there.

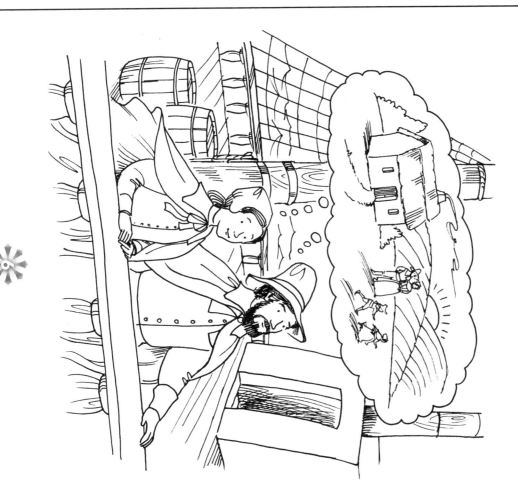

The Pilgrims did not go to the king's church. They held secret meetings in their own homes. Soon, the king found out about the meetings. He sent many of the Pilgrims to jail.

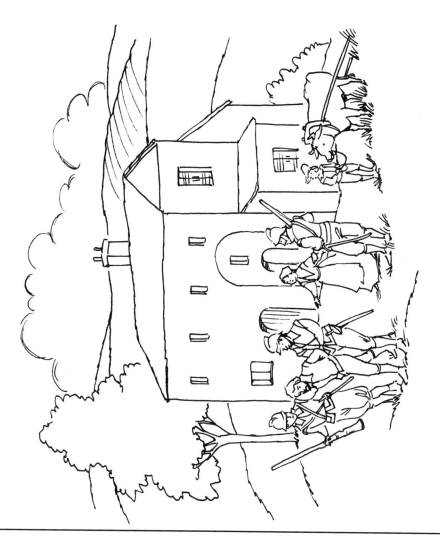

It was against the law not to belong to the Church of England.

Hello, America!

The Pilgrims decided to sail to America. In this new land, they would be free to follow their own faith. They could also own land and live as they pleased.

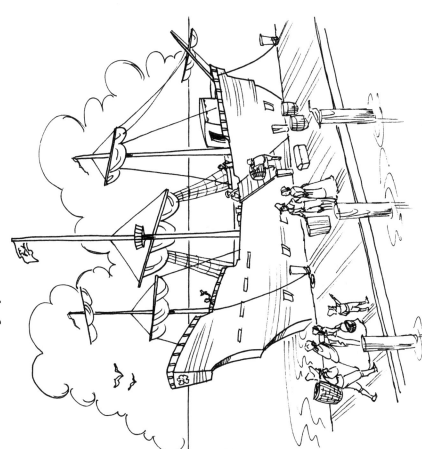

The Pilgrims sailed to America on the *Mayflower*.

Off to Holland

Some Pilgrims wanted to leave England. They moved to Holland. There they could follow their own beliefs.

The Pilgrims stayed in Holland for 12 years. They worked hard and grew tired. They missed their English way of life, but they could not move back to England.

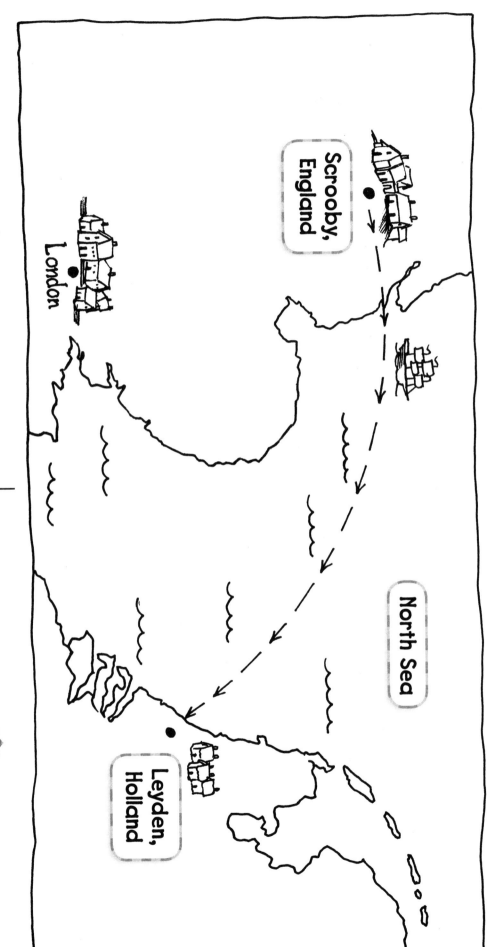

Scrooby, England

London

North Sea

Leyden, Holland

Voyage on the Mayflower

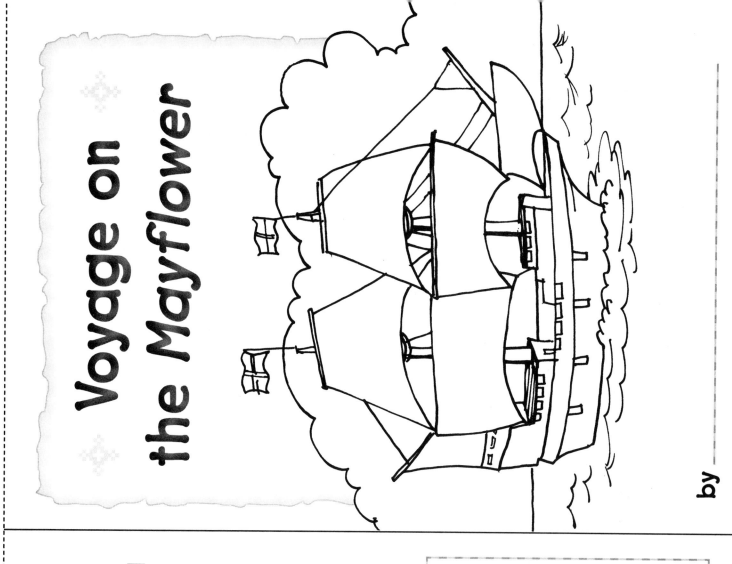

by _____

On the Mayflower

The voyage on the *Mayflower* was an adventure. Many things happened to the Pilgrims on their trip. Write something that you learned about their voyage. Then draw a picture.

_____

_____

_____

_____

A Ship Sets Sail

In 1620, the *Mayflower* set sail from England. There were 102 Pilgrims on the small ship. It was crowded, but they wanted to make the trip. They were going to a new land!

Pilgrims

Mayflower

The Pilgrims were happy to see the shore. They were ready to make their home in a new land.

What ocean did the Pilgrims cross on the *Mayflower*?

Plymouth, England

Atlantic Ocean

Land Ho!

Finally, the Pilgrims reached the new land. The trip took 66 days.

Cape Cod, Massachusetts

A Stormy Trip

The *Mayflower* sailed through many storms. Strong winds blew the ship. High waves rocked it from side to side. The Pilgrims were tossed around on the ship.

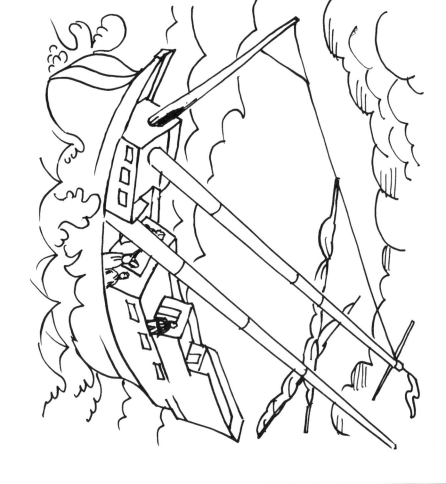

Living on the ship wasn't easy. The Pilgrims got wet and cold. Many got seasick.

It was not safe to cook with a fire. The Pilgrims had to eat hard crackers, salted meat, and cheese.

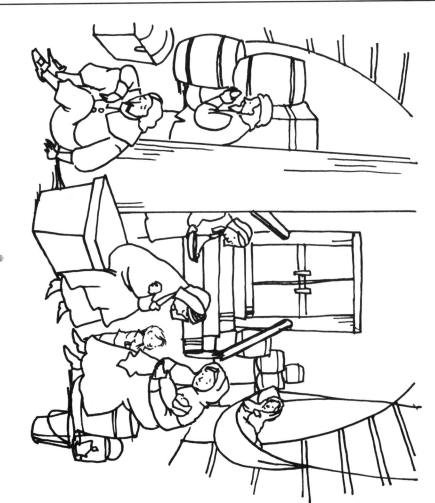

Meet Squanto

by _____

A Helping Hand

Write about one way that Squanto helped the Pilgrims. Then draw a picture.

_____

_____

_____

_____

_____

Squanto was a Native American. He lived near the Pilgrims' settlement. Squanto knew how to speak English. The Pilgrims were happy that he spoke their language!

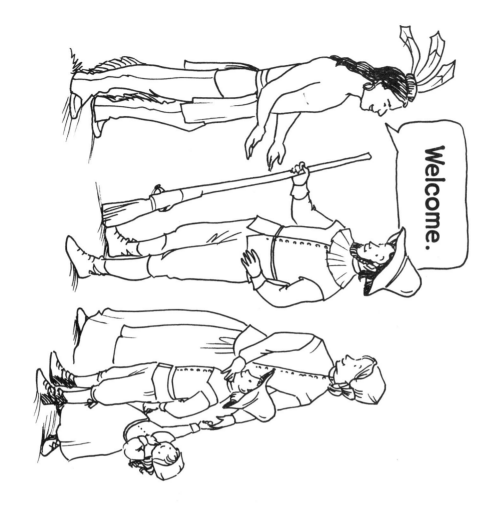

Welcome.

Squanto spoke English and the language of the Wampanoag. He helped the Pilgrims and Native Americans talk to each other. The Pilgrims were grateful for the many ways that Squanto helped them.

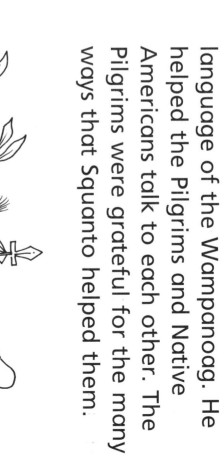

Squanto was a translator. He helped the Pilgrims and Wampanoag make a peace treaty.

The Pilgrims had a lot to learn about making a living in their new homeland. Squanto taught them many things. He showed them how to hunt for deer, turkey, and other animals.

Squanto taught the Pilgrims where to find wild berries. He showed them which plants were safe to eat. He also taught them how to get sap from maple trees. The sap was used to make sugar.

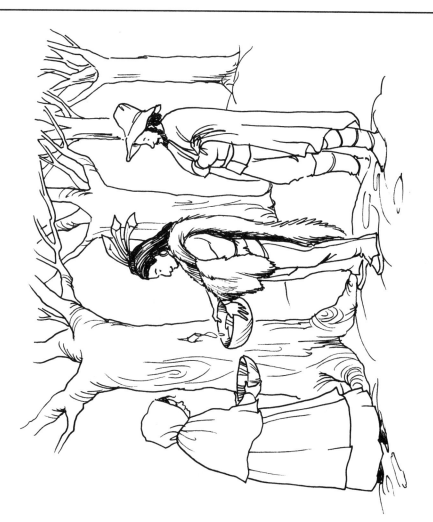

Maple sap was boiled down and made into sugar.

Squanto was a good fisherman. He helped the Pilgrims find the best fishing places. He showed them how to catch fish and eels. He taught them how to dig for and cook clams.

A clambake on the beach.

The Pilgrims had trouble growing plants. Squanto taught them to plant small fish in the ground with corn seeds. The fish made the corn grow better. He also taught the Pilgrims how to grow beans, squash, and other foods.

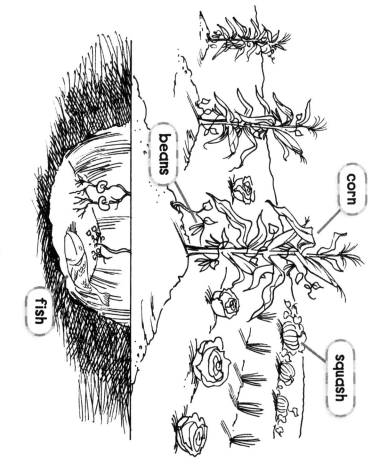

beans

corn

fish

squash

Fish is a fertilizer that helps crops grow.

Life in a Pilgrim Village

by _____

Fun Fact!

Write an interesting fact about Pilgrim life. Then draw a picture.

_____

_____

_____

_____

Homes

Pilgrim houses had one main room used for eating, sleeping, and living. The homes were made of wood boards. They had thatched, or straw, roofs. Pilgrims made their beds from straw, too.

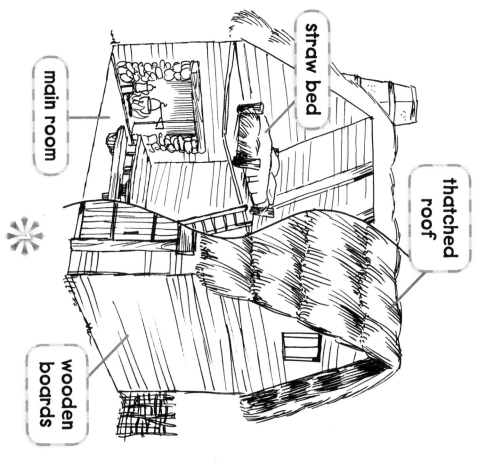

main room

straw bed

thatched roof

wooden boards

Fun and Games

Pilgrim children enjoyed footraces and hide-and-seek. Another favorite game was marbles. They probably played with toys such as hoops, tops, and pinwheels. Children also liked to say tongue twisters and tell riddles.

knicker box

marbles

Meals

Pilgrims ate goose, duck, deer, rabbit, pig, fish, and shellfish. They cooked meat, vegetables, and stews over a fire. Bread and pies were baked in an outdoor oven. Pilgrims ate their biggest meal in the middle of the day.

Clothes

The Pilgrims brought clothes with them from England. They also made their own clothes. Both men and women wore many layers. Boys and girls wore dresses until age 6 or 7. Older boys wore breeches, or short pants.

Chores

All of the Pilgrims worked hard. The children often helped take care of the animals and worked in the fields. They also gathered firewood and fetched water. Some helped with the cooking and watched the younger children.

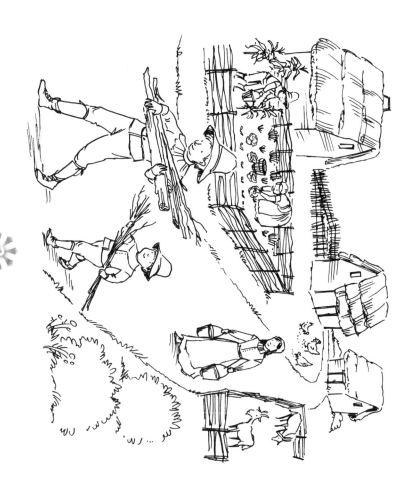

School

There were no schools in the Pilgrim's village. Some parents taught their children how to read and write at home.

Do you think many Pilgrim children would have wanted to go to school? Why or why not?

_____

_____

_____

horn book

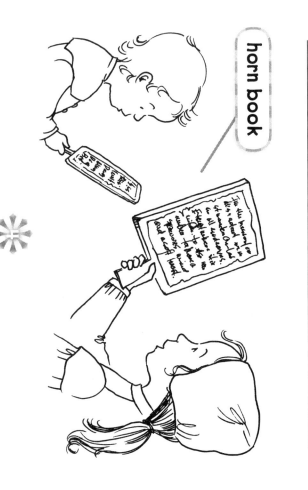

Life in a
Wampanoag
Homesite

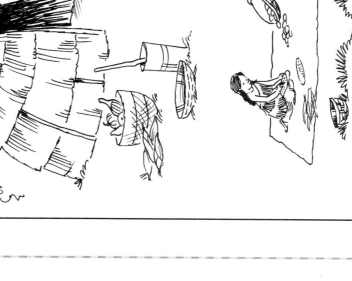

by _____

Fun Fact!

Write an interesting fact about Wampanoag life. Then draw a picture.

_____
_____
_____
_____

Homes

The Wampanoag lived in wetus most of the year. Wetus were made of curved poles. They were covered with tree bark or grass. A fire pit was built inside the home. Families slept on mats made of animal fur.

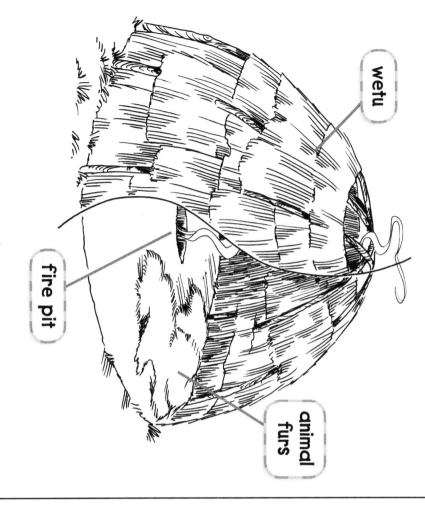

wetu

fire pit

animal furs

Fun and Games

Wampanoag children played in ways that helped them grow strong. They enjoyed swimming, running races, and playing toss-and-catch games. The children also liked to dance, make music, and listen to stories.

Meals

The women cooked meals outdoors over a fire. The Wampanoag ate goose, duck, turkey, rabbit, squirrel, deer, and seafood. They grew corn, squash, beans, and other vegetables. They also ate cranberries and nuts.

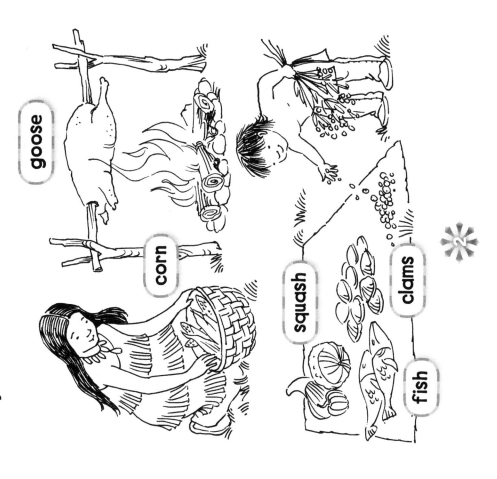

goose

corn

squash

clams

fish

Clothes

The Wampanoag wore clothes and shoes made from deerskin. Males wore a cloth around their waists. Females wore dresses. They often carried a pouch filled with dried corn. The Wampanoag made jewelry from bones, stones, and shells.

jewelry

pouch

loincloth

leggings

moccasins

Chores

Learning to hunt and fish was the main job of Wampanoag boys. They also made their own arrows. The girls helped cook, gather shellfish, make clothes, and watch over the crops. Children also helped fetch water and gather firewood.

School

The Wampanoag did not have schools. The men taught the boys how to hunt and fish. Girls learned how to prepare and cook food from the women.

Explain how everyday life was like school for Wampanoag children.

_____

_____

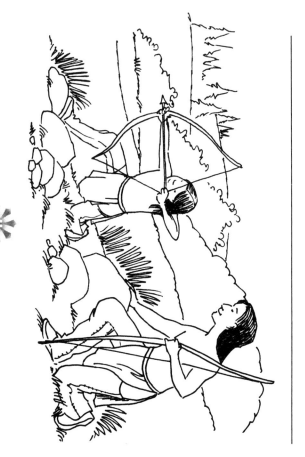

The First Thanksgiving

by _____

A Feast to Remember

Write what you learned about the First Thanksgiving. Then draw a picture.

_____

_____

_____

_____

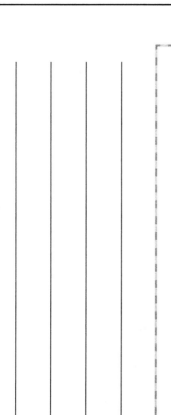

The Pilgrims had a long, stormy voyage to America. Then they faced a cold winter. The weather made it hard to build homes and find food. The Pilgrims were hungry and sick. Many of them died.

Half of the Pilgrims died by the end of winter.

The men had shooting contests. The Pilgrims marched in a parade. There was music, dancing, and singing. What a celebration!

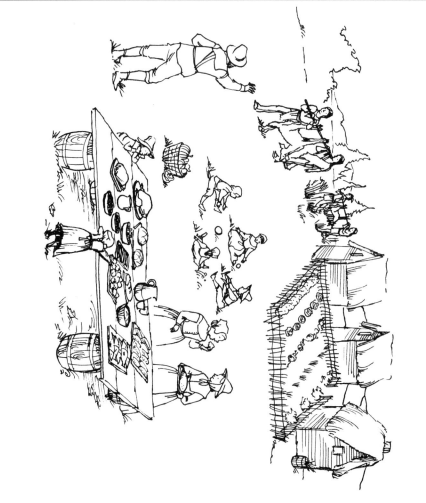

The first harvest feast is now known as the First Thanksgiving. It lasted three days!

Finally, spring came. The Pilgrims cleared land for their crops. A helpful Native American named Squanto taught them how to hunt and grow food. He also helped them make friends with the Wampanoag people.

The Pilgrims cleared about 20 acres for planting.

A group of Wampanoag men joined the celebration. They brought five deer for the feast. The Pilgrims and their Wampanoag friends ate, drank, and visited with each other. They also played games and ran races.

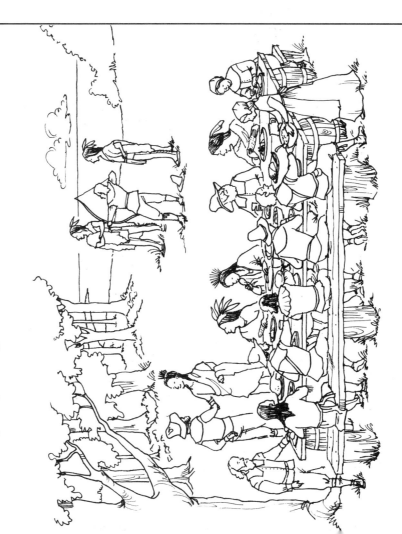

About 50 Pilgrims and 90 Wampanoag were at the feast.

By fall, the Pilgrims had built seven houses and a meeting place. At harvest time, they had plenty of corn to store for later. They also stored meat, fruit, and other vegetables. No one would starve this winter!

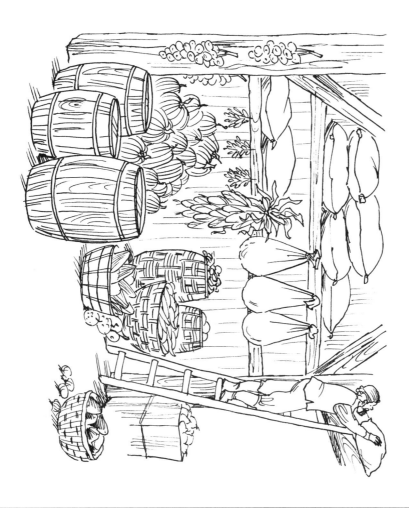

Meat was salted and vegetables were dried for later use.

The Pilgrims were thankful for their homes, food, and friends! They decided to celebrate their first harvest with a feast. The men hunted duck and geese. The women and children made breads, pies, stews, and other dishes.

The Pilgrims also caught fish, eels, and shellfish for the feast.

A Thanksgiving Meal: 1621 and Today

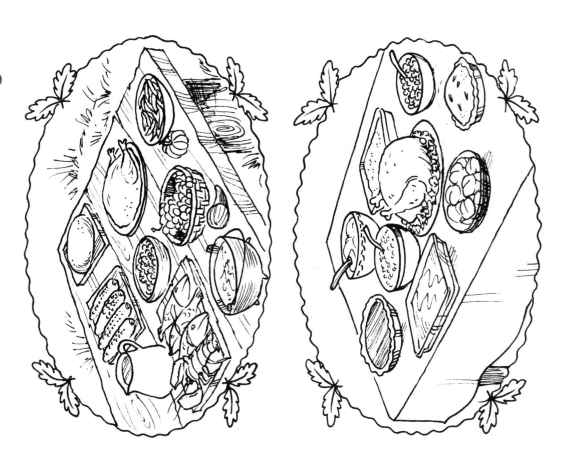

by _____

Compare and Contrast

Write one way that today's Thanksgiving meal is different from the feast in 1621.

_____

_____

_____

_____

_____

_____

Write one way that today's Thanksgiving meal is the same as the feast in 1621.

_____

_____

_____

_____

_____

_____

Meat and Fish

1621

The Pilgrims and Wampanoag ate duck, geese, turkey, and deer at the First Thanksgiving. They had fish, lobster, and clams, too. These foods were usually cooked over a fire.

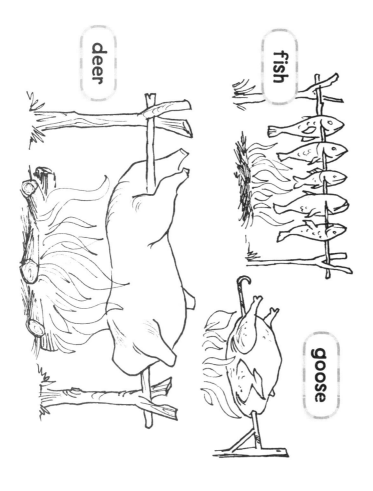

fish

goose

deer

Most meat was cooked on a spit over an open fire.

Today

Pies, cakes, and other desserts are a big part of today's Thanksgiving meals. What is your favorite Thanksgiving pie?

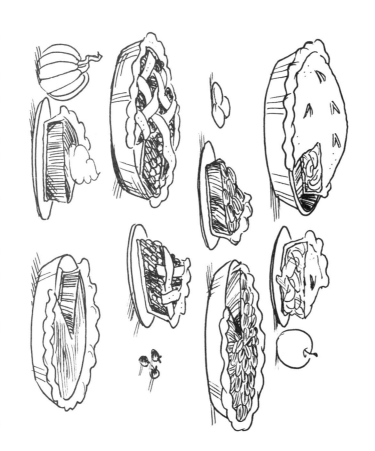

The Pilgrims did not have the ingredients to make pie crusts like we enjoy today.

Today

Today, turkey is the traditional Thanksgiving meat. Most people roast turkey in an oven. Some cook it in a deep fryer. Often, ham, chicken, and seafood are also part of the meal.

The pilgrims did not have ovens at the First Thanksgiving.

Sweets and Desserts

1621

The Pilgrims did not have sugar to make sweet pies and desserts at the First Thanksgiving. The sweetest dishes on the table were probably wild berries and dishes made with them.

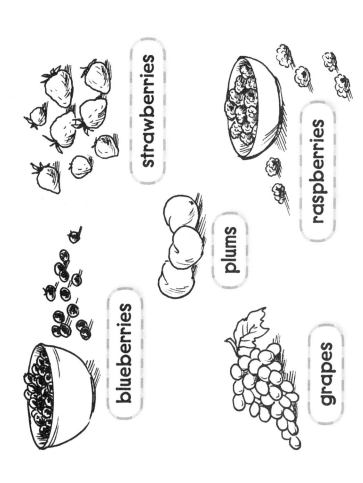

strawberries

blueberries

plums

raspberries

grapes

Pilgrims dried fruit after picking it so they could eat it later in the year.

Fruits and Vegetables

1621

The Pilgrims grew most of the food served at the First Thanksgiving. They had corn, squash, beans, carrots, and spinach. They also served stews, pumpkin pudding, and fried cornbread.

The Pilgrims also enjoyed wild berries and nuts at the meal.

Today

Many kinds of fruits and vegetables are served today at Thanksgiving. We enjoy green beans, corn, cranberry sauce, potatoes, and applesauce. We buy most of our foods from grocery stores and farmers' markets.

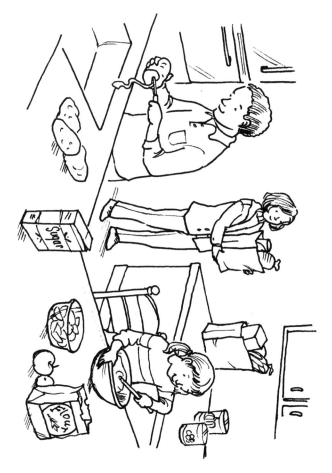

Potatoes and apples were not grown in America at the time of the First Thanksgiving.

Our Thanksgiving Holiday

by _____

Thanksgiving is rich in history and tradition. Write about your favorite Thanksgiving tradition. Then draw a picture.

_____
_____
_____
_____

In the Early Days

Thanksgiving Day was not always a holiday in our country. After the Pilgrims' First Thanksgiving, days for giving thanks were celebrated at different times in different places.

Days of Thanksgiving

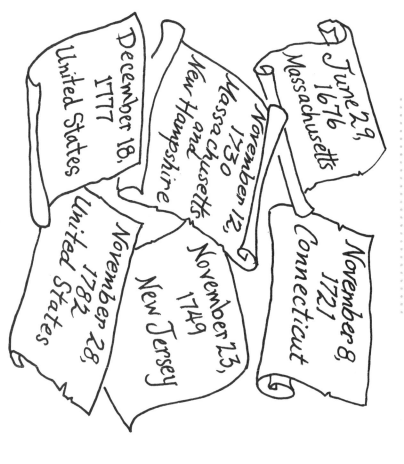

June 29, 1676
Massachusetts

November 12, 1730
Massachusetts and New Hampshire

November 8, 1721
Connecticut

November 23, 1749
New Jersey

December 18, 1777
United States

November 28, 1782
United States

In 1924, Macy's Department Store in New York City held its first Thanksgiving Day Parade. Today, people everywhere watch the parade on TV. Many also enjoy watching football on Thanksgiving Day.

Animals were in the first Macy's Thanksgiving Day parade. Today, giant balloons float over the parade.

President George Washington called for a day of Thanksgiving in 1789. He set aside the last Thursday in November for this special day. In later years, some presidents called for days of Thanksgiving and some did not.

November 26, 1789 will be a day of Thanksgiving for our country.

Traditions and Symbols

The cornucopia has become a symbol of Thanksgiving. A cornucopia is a basket shaped like a horn. It is filled with vegetables, fruit, and grains. Turkeys and pumpkins are also Thanksgiving symbols.

Cornucopia means "horn of plenty" and is a symbol of the harvest.

A National Holiday

For many years, a writer named Sarah Hale wrote to every president. She wanted Thanksgiving to be a national holiday. Finally, in 1863, Abraham Lincoln made the last Thursday in November a national day of Thanksgiving!

The country celebrated Thanksgiving on the last Thursday of November for many years.

In 1939, Franklin Roosevelt moved Thanksgiving to a week earlier in November. Many did not like the change, and they let the President know! The date was moved back to the last Thursday of the month in 1941.

In 1941, Congress made Thanksgiving a permanent holiday. It would be celebrated every year on the 4th Thursday in November.

Giving Thanks

by _____

At Thanksgiving, what do you give thanks for? Write three things and draw a picture for each one.

At Thanksgiving, we give thanks for the many good things in our lives. We are thankful for the special people we know and what they mean to us.

I am thankful for this person in my life:

We are thankful for the many things in nature.

sun, moon, and stars

plants and trees

animals and insects

weather

I am thankful for this thing in nature:

We are thankful for the things that we enjoy.

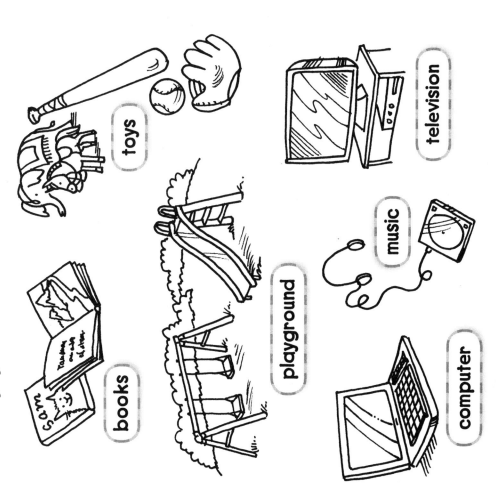

books

toys

playground

television

music

computer

I am thankful for this thing that I need:

_____

We are thankful for the things we need.

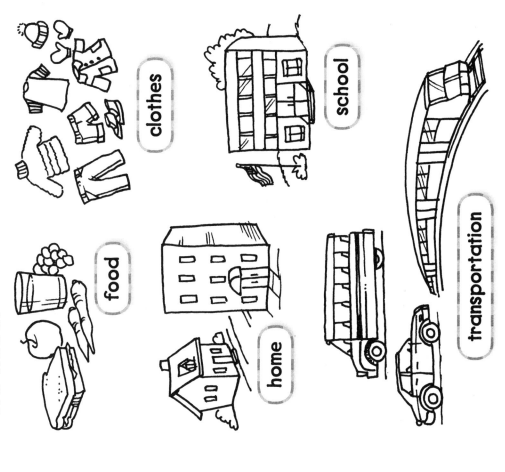

clothes

school

food

home

transportation

I am thankful to have this thing that I need:

_____

We are thankful for our community.

I am thankful for this part of my community:

We are thankful for being able to help others around us.

clean up

pick up trash

donate food

visit the elderly

donate clothes

I am thankful that I can help others in this way:

My Thanksgiving Day

by _____

Three things I like most about my Thanksgiving are. . . .

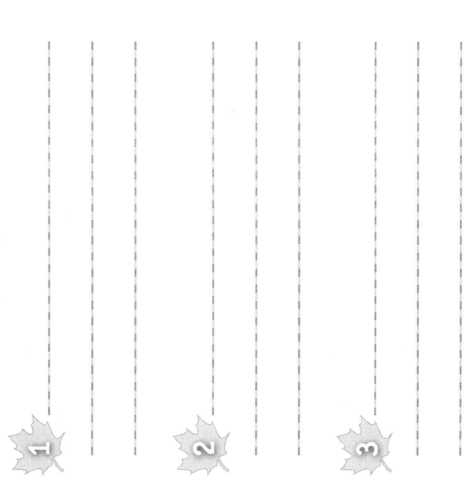

1 _____
_____
_____

2 _____
_____
_____

3 _____
_____
_____

Now, draw a picture of your Thanksgiving on the cover.

Where I Celebrate

Families and friends gather in many places to celebrate Thanksgiving. Where do you celebrate?

_____

Draw a picture of that place.

I Help and Share

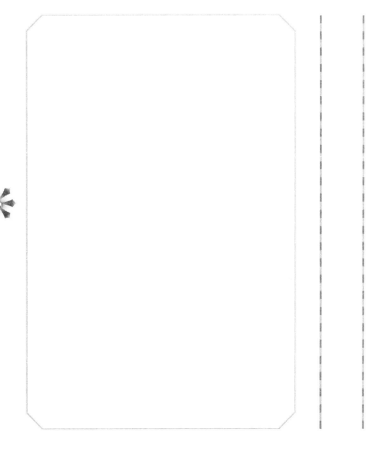

People often share with and help others on Thanksgiving. Some help prepare a meal. Others share their belongings. Write about how you help or share on this day. Then draw a picture.

My Family and Friends

Many people celebrate Thanksgiving with family, friends, and neighbors. I celebrate with:

_____

_____

Draw a picture of some of these people.

I Have Fun

On Thanksgiving, many people play games, watch parades and football, and enjoy the outdoors. Write about what you do for fun. Then draw a picture.

_____

_____

My Thanksgiving Meal

Thanksgiving is a time to make and enjoy delicious foods. Name some of the foods that you eat at Thanksgiving. Draw some of your favorites.

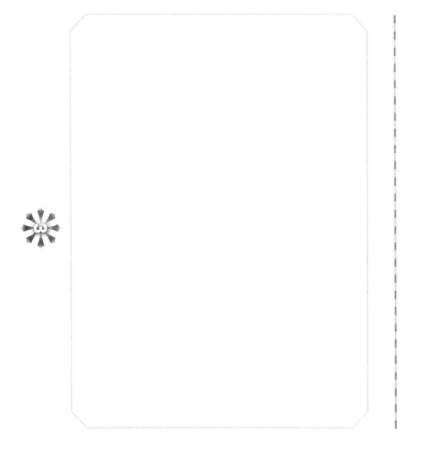

I Give Thanks

People give thanks for many things at Thanksgiving. List some things that you are thankful for. Then draw a picture.